World Series HEROES

BY
RICHARD DEITSCH

A SPORTS ILLUSTRATED FOR KIDS Book

Contents

Great Players 4
Great Teams 22
Great Moments 27

Heroes come in all sizes: Joe Morgan (above), Rollie Fingers (top), and Babe Ruth and Lou Gehrig

INTRODUCTION

Ever since Cy Young and the Boston Pilgrims defeated the Pittsburgh Pirates in 1903, the champions of the National League and American League have met to determine the best team in baseball. It has been an annual event since 1905. In 1996, the New York Yankees won the 92nd World Series!

The "Fall Classic," as the Series is called, has produced many heroes, from big boppers like Babe Ruth to tiny terrors like Kirby Puckett.

The Series has given us some of the most exciting moments in sports history, too. Did you see Toronto star Joe Carter hit his ninth-inning homer to win the 1993 Series? Have you heard about Don Larsen's perfect game or Willie Mays's amazing catch? Did you cheer for Tom Glavine and the Atlanta Braves in 1995?

World Series Heroes has sections on the best players, the greatest teams, and the most magical moments in Series history. When the next World Series comes around, you'll be the expert!

Great teams: The Yankees went wild after they won their 23rd Series, in '96.

Great players: Kirby Puckett (left) and Tom Glavine

Babe Ruth

The Sultan of Swat was a pitcher too

Everyone knows Babe Ruth hit home runs. He hit some of his best in the World Series. But did you know he was a Series pitching hero, too? Babe is the only player to star in the Series as a both pitcher and a hitter.

Babe pitched for the Boston Red Sox in the 1916 and 1918 Series. He had a 3–0 record and a 0.87 earned run average. His streak of 29 1/3 straight scoreless innings was a Series record for 43 years! Boston won both Series.

But Babe's greatest fame came as a Yankee slugger. He hit .347 in seven Series for New York. He is the only player to hit three homers in a single Series game twice.

No question, Babe was terrific. Was he so good he could "call" a home run? In Game 3 of the 1932 Series, Babe came up in the fifth inning with the score tied. Some Chicago Cubs players yelled at him. He yelled back. Cub pitcher Charlie Root started yelling. Suddenly, Babe pointed in Charlie's direction. No one knows if he was pointing at Charlie or the outfield fence. But he smacked the next pitch into the bleachers. Babe laughed out loud as he circled the bases. Another home run for the Sultan of Swat!

EXTRA INNINGS

double trouble Babe and Lou were an awesome combination. In 1927, Babe smashed 60 home runs and Lou drove in 175 runs — both records. The Yankees won 110 games!

one-man team Babe twice hit more home runs in a season than any other *team* in the A.L. He hit 54 homers in 1920 and 60 in 1927.

Scouting REPORT

name George Herman Ruth
born February 6, 1895, Baltimore, Maryland
died August 16, 1948
career stats Hit .342 with 714 homers and 2,211 RBIs over 22 seasons (1914–35) with three teams. Second in career homers and RBIs. Won 94 games as a pitcher.
world series stats Hit .326 with 15 homers and 33 RBIs in 10 Series. Hit .625 in the 1928 Series.

Babe (above and right) and Lou led New York to many Series titles.

Lou Gehrig

He quietly drove in a run a game

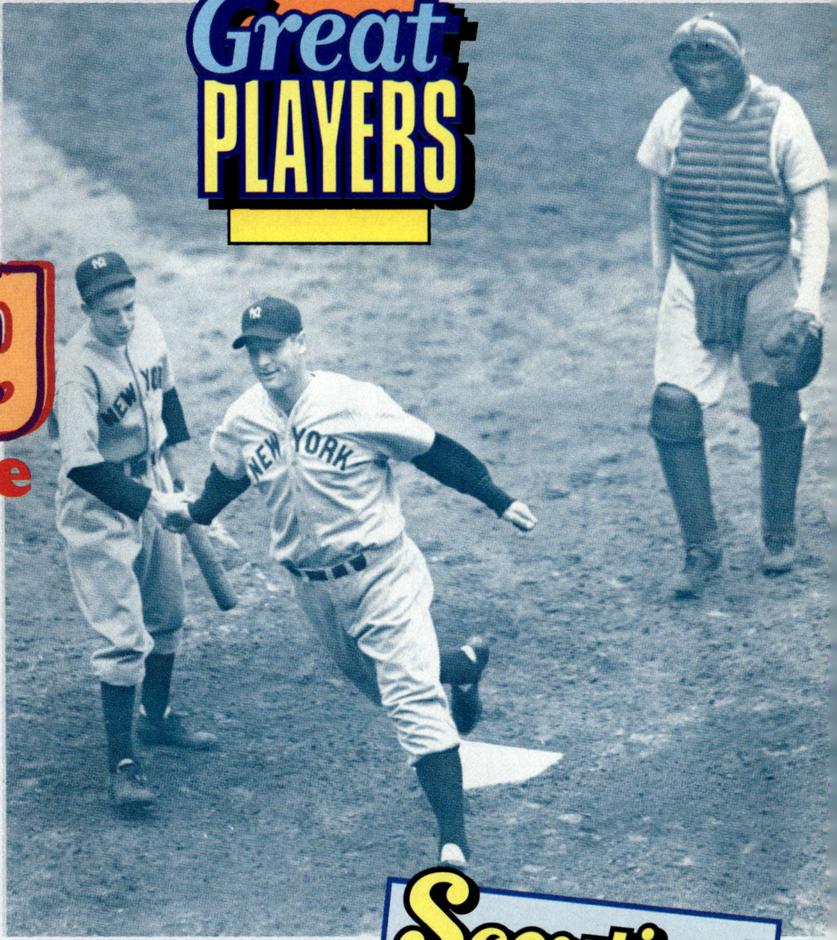

Lou teamed with Joe DiMaggio (above, left) and Babe to win the Series

Lou Gehrig played much of his career in the huge shadow cast by his Yankee teammate Babe Ruth. But Lou cast a pretty big shadow himself — especially when it came to the World Series!

In seven Series, Lou played 34 games and drove in 35 runs. That's more than one RBI per game! In the four Series that Lou and Babe played together, Lou had a higher batting average (.422 to .409) and drove in more runs (25 to 22) than Babe.

Lou's greatest Series show came in 1928, when New York beat the St. Louis Cardinals in four games. He batted .545, with four home runs and nine RBIs. No one else, not even Babe, ever hit four home runs in a four-game Series.

In 1932, Lou hit .529, with three home runs and eight RBIs, as the Yankees swept the Chicago Cubs in four games. The Yankees won six of the seven Series that Lou played in.

The Yanks could always count on Lou. On June 1, 1925, he pinch-hit. The next day, Lou started at first base. He played in every game for the next 14 seasons! By the time the streak ended, in 1939, Lou had played in 2,130 consecutive games!

Scouting REPORT

name Henry Louis Gehrig
born June 19, 1903, New York, New York.
died June 2, 1941
career stats Hit .340 with 493 homers and 1,990 RBIs over 17 seasons (1923–39) with the Yankees. Named A.L. MVP twice. Won the Triple Crown in 1934.
world series stats Hit .361 with 10 homers and 35 RBIs in seven Series. Fourth all-time in RBIs and slugging percentage.
fast fact Lou wasn't known for his speed, but he stole home 15 times in his career.

Mickey Mantle

The Yankee star was the Series' greatest slugger

If performing under pressure is the real test of an athlete's talent, then Mickey Mantle was the best player in baseball history. No one played better in baseball's pressure cooker — the World Series — than Mickey.

The New York Yankee slugger hit 18 home runs in the World Series, more than any other player. He drove in more runs (40) than anyone else. He scored more runs (42). Mickey holds or shares 17 Series batting records! With his help, the Yankees won seven world championships between 1951 and 1962.

Mickey did not just hit home runs. He launched them out of ballparks as if he were aiming for the moon. Mickey had at least one home run in nine of the 12 World Series he played in. He hit his first one in the 1952 Series, when he was 20 years old.

Mickey hit many key homers, but here are two:

● **1953 World Series, Game 5:** The Series against the Brooklyn Dodgers was tied at two games each. With the bases loaded and two out, Mickey hit a third-inning grand slam to spark

Mickey shared Yankee Stadium's centerfield with monuments to past stars.

Scouting REPORT

name Mickey Charles Mantle
born October 20, 1931, Spavinaw, Oklahoma
died August 13, 1995
career stats Hit .298 with 536 homers and 1,509 RBIs over 18 seasons (1951–68) with the Yankees. Elected to the Hall of Fame, 1974. Eighth all-time in homers. Three-time A.L. MVP.
world series stats Hit .257 (59 for 230) with 18 home runs and 40 RBIs in 12 Series. Holds Series record for most home runs, most RBIs, and most runs scored in a career.
fast fact Mickey hit three home runs in three different World Series.

Great PLAYERS

Mighty Mickey: Nobody hit more home runs in the World Series than New York's super centerfielder. He hit 18, including this one in the 1958 Series.

the Yankees to an 11–7 victory. They won the Series the next day.

• **1964 World Series, Game 3:** The Yankees and the St. Louis Cardinals were tied, 1–1. Mickey led off the bottom of the ninth and blasted reliever Barney Schultz's first pitch into the rightfield stands. The home run won the game. It also moved Mickey into first place on the all-time World Series home-run list. (It was Mickey's 16th career Series homer. Babe Ruth had held the record with 15.)

The 1964 Series was Mickey's last. He was 32 years old and was suffering from a decade of knee and leg injuries. But he could still hit the ball. Although the Yankees lost the Series, Mickey led all hitters with three homers and eight RBIs.

Mickey wasn't just a home-run hitter. He was an outstanding centerfielder, too. In Game 2 of the 1956 World Series, Mickey made a dazzling play. He raced into deep left-centerfield and made a backhanded catch of a long drive hit by the Dodgers Gil Hodges. The catch helped save Yankee pitcher Don Larsen's perfect game, a 2–0 victory (see page 28).

Oh, yes, Mickey homered in that game, too.

EXTRA INNINGS

all-around crown In baseball, a player wins the Triple Crown when he leads his league in batting, home runs, and RBIs. Only nine players in history have done that. Mickey did it in 1956. He led the A.L. with a .353 batting average, 52 homers, and 130 RBIs.

both ways Mickey was one of the best switch-hitters in history. He hit homers from both sides of the plate in the same game 10 times.

long ball Mickey hit *long* home runs. Against Detroit in 1960, he hit a ball clear out of Tiger Stadium. The ball landed in a lumberyard across the street from the ballpark, about 600 feet away!

two-fer Mickey hit two home runs in one World Series game twice, in 1958 and in 1960.

7

Bob Gibson

The Cardinal ace owned home plate

Great PLAYERS

Bob Gibson of the St. Louis Cardinals pitched as if he owned home plate. He would glare at batters. He would throw his fastball on the inside of the plate (near the batter) to let hitters know that he was in charge. He was one of the most intimidating pitchers in baseball history — especially when a championship was on the line.

Bob lost his first World Series start, to the New York Yankees in the 1964 Series. But he won the next seven World Series games he started, pitching a complete game each time. It took nearly four years before the Detroit Tigers broke Bob's World Series winning streak, in Game 7 of the 1968 Series.

In the 1967 Series against the Boston Red Sox, Bob was nearly unhittable. He won three games and struck out 26 in 27 innings. In the key seventh game, he gave up three hits and struck out 10!

Although the Cards lost the 1968 Series, Bob's performance in Game 1 was one of the greatest in World Series history. He set a Series record with 17 strikeouts and allowed just five hits. The Cards won, 4–0. Bob had 35 strikeouts and a measly 1.35 earned run in the Series.

He owned home plate, and batters knew it!

Bob blew batters away with his fastball and his mean glare.

Scouting REPORT

name Robert "Gibby" Gibson
born November 9, 1935, Omaha, Nebraska
career stats Won 251 games, lost 174, with a 2.91 ERA for St. Louis over 17 seasons (1959–75). Set modern-day record (300 innings or more) for best ERA in a season (1.12).
world series stats 7–2 with a 1.89 ERA in three Series. Holds six World Series pitching records, including most strikeouts in a game (17).

EXTRA INNINGS

what a year In 1968, Bob was 22–9 with a 1.12 ERA. He had 268 strikeouts and 13 shutouts. He won the N.L.'s Cy Young and MVP awards.

K korner Bob struck out 92 batters in 81 World Series innings. Only New York Yankee Whitey Ford has more total Series strikeouts. He has 94, but he pitched 65 more innings!

Mickey Lolich

The surprise hero won three games

Mickey outpitched Bob Gibson to lead the Tigers over the Cards in 1968.

Many people expected a pitcher to be the hero of the 1968 World Series. They just didn't think the pitcher would be Mickey Lolich.

Mickey's teammate Denny McClain had won an amazing 31 games during the 1968 season. Bob Gibson of the St. Louis Cardinals (left) had set a major league earned run average. One of them might be the star. Not Mickey.

But Mickey fooled everyone. First, he won Game 2. Then, he won Game 5. Even after that, Mickey wasn't expected to win Game 7. He was pitching against Bob, who had won seven World Series games in a row!

As expected, the game was tight. It was scoreless after five innings. Then speedy Lou Brock led off the sixth inning for the Cardinals with a single. But Mickey picked Lou off first. One out later, Cardinal Curt Flood singled to short. Again, Mickey picked off the base runner! St. Louis didn't score in the inning.

The Tigers scored three runs in the next inning. They added another in the ninth. Mickey kept the Cards under control. He gave up only five hits and just one run. The Tigers won, 4–1! It was Mickey's third complete-game victory.

Only six pitchers have won three games in a single World Series. Mickey, the Tigers' unlikely hero, is one of them!

Scouting REPORT

name Michael Stephen "Mickey" Lolich

born September 12, 1940, Portland, Oregon

career stats Won 217 and lost 191 with a 3.44 ERA over 16 seasons (1963–79) with the Tigers, Mets, and Padres.

world series stats 3–0 with five earned runs, 21 strikeouts, and a 1.67 ERA over 27 innings in one Series.

fast fact In 1971, Mickey led the A.L. in wins (25), strikeouts, and complete games. But he didn't win the Cy Young Award! Oakland's Vida Blue won with 24 wins and a 1.82 ERA.

Brooks Robinson

Great PLAYERS

The "human vacuum cleaner" swept up the Cincinnati Reds

Brooks Robinson of the Baltimore Orioles played such awesome defense during the 1970 World Series that he earned himself a new nickname. The new nickname was "Mr. Hoover." Hoover was the brand name of a popular vacuum cleaner. The Cincinnati Reds said Brooks was like a vacuum cleaner because he scooped up everything that was hit anywhere near third base.

Brooks was one of the best all-around third basemen in baseball history. His performance in the 1970 World Series, between the Orioles and the Reds, though, was beyond best. It was amazing. Time after time, Brooks robbed the Reds of hits with his great fielding. He was no slouch at the plate either. Thanks in large part to "Mr. Hoover," the Orioles won the Series in five games.

Brooks's defensive magic started in the opening game of the Series. With

SCOUTING REPORT

name Brooks Calbert Robinson
born May 18, 1937, Little Rock, Arkansas
career stats Hit .267 with 268 homers and 1,357 RBIs over 23 seasons (1955–77) with the Baltimore Orioles. Elected to the Hall of Fame in 1983. All-time major league leader in assists, putouts, double plays, and fielding percentage by a third baseman. Won 16 Gold Gloves in a row!
world series stats Hit .263 (20 for 76) with three home runs and 14 RBIs in four Series. Hit .429 with two homers and six RBIs in 1970. Named Series MVP.
cool fact After the 1971 season, Brooks sent the glove he used in the 1970 Series to the Baseball Hall of Fame in Cooperstown, New York.

the score tied 3–3 in the bottom of the sixth inning, Cincinnati's Lee May hit a hard smash to third. It looked like a sure double. But Brooks ranged far to his right and made a backhand stop. He then spun around from foul territory and fired a throw to first. Lee couldn't believe it. Brooks had thrown him out! In the next inning, Brooks hit a home run to give the Orioles a 4–3 victory.

In Game 3, Brooks made great plays in the first, second, and sixth innings. The Orioles won easily, 9–3. In Game 4, he had another amazing day. He had four hits, including a home run, in four times at-bat. But the Reds hung tough to win, 6–5.

Baltimore won again the next day, 9–3, to lock up the world championship. Brooks was named

EXTRA INNINGS

great glove Brooks led the A.L. in fielding percentage a record 11 times.

he's on third Brooks played more games (2,870) at third base than any other player in baseball history.

mvp Brooks was named the A.L. MVP in 1964. That season, he hit .317 with 28 home runs and 118 RBIs.

mauling minnesota Brooks hit an astounding .583 (7 for 12) against the Minnesota Twins in the 1970 A. L. championship series. The Orioles swept the Twins in three games (It was a best-of-five series).

Right, left, or center, Brooks stopped everything that came anywhere near third base during the 1970 Series.

Most Valuable Player of the Series. In addition to his standout defensive play, he batted .429 and led the Orioles with six RBIs.

Brooks had played in two previous World Series. In 1966, he helped the Orioles sweep the Los Angeles Dodgers. But in 1969, against the New York Mets, Brooks had only 1 hit in 19 at-bats. Baltimore lost in five games. In 1970, Brooks was determined to lead his team to victory. He even put a sign on his luggage during the season that said: "Brooks Robinson, 1970 World Champions."

With his defensive magic and hot hitting, Brooks made that prediction come true.

Great PLAYERS

Reggie Jackson
Mr. October delivered in the clutch

Mr. October. What kind of a nickname is that? It's the kind you give a player who plays his very best when the pressure is on and the World Series is up for grabs. It's the kind of nickname you give Reggie Jackson.

Reggie liked being in the spotlight. He seemed to shine when the lights were brightest — during the World Series, in October. "I love to hit when the pressure is on," said Reggie.

Reggie played for five World Series-winning teams. While he was with the Oakland A's, they won three straight championships, from 1972 to 1974 (see page 25). Reggie was named Most Valuable Player of the 1973 Series.

But Reggie is best remembered for what he did in the 1977 World Series, when he was playing for the New York Yankees. In the sixth game of that Series, against the Los Angeles Dodgers, Reggie did something that only one other player in baseball history had ever done. He hit three home runs. Babe Ruth is the only other player to have hit three homers in one Series game.

What a night Reggie had! He was feeling confident. He had hit two home runs in earlier games, and the Yankees were just one win away

from winning the championship.

In the fourth inning, Reggie came to bat against Dodger pitcher Burt Hooton. On Burt's first pitch, Reggie hit a two-run homer to give the Yankees a 4–3 lead.

Reggie batted again in the fifth inning, against reliever Elias Sosa. Again, he drove the first pitch into the rightfield stands for a two-run blast!

In the eighth inning, Reggie batted once more. The crowd at Yankee Stadium was on its feet. "Reg-GIE, Reg-GIE," they chanted. Could Reggie do it again? Dodger pitcher Charlie Hough threw a tricky pitch. Reggie hit it solidly. He sent it 450 feet into the centerfield stands. The crowd went wild.

Reggie had hit three home runs on three straight pitches thrown by three different pitchers. He had knocked in five runs and led the Yankees to an 8–4 victory to clinch the World Series title.

Mr. October had come through!

Scouting REPORT

name Reginald Martinez "Reggie" Jackson
born May 18, 1946, Wyncote, Pennsylvania
career stats Hit .262 with 563 home runs and 1,702 RBIs over 21 seasons (1967–87) with five teams. Elected to the Hall of Fame, 1993. Sixth on the all-time homer list. A.L. MVP in 1973.
world series Hit .357 (35 for 98) with 10 homers and 24 RBIs in five Series. Only four players have hit more World Series homers in their careers.
cool fact Reggie had a candy bar named after him.

EXTRA INNINGS

winning colors Reggie played on 10 first-place teams and five World Series winners over a 12-year period (1971–82).
super series In the 1977 World Series, Reggie broke or tied 10 records, including most home runs (5) and highest slugging percentage (.755). He batted an amazing .450 with eight RBIs. He won his second World Series MVP award.
most valuable Reggie was named the MVP of the 1973 World Series, when his Oakland A's won their second of three straight championships. Reggie hit .310 (9 for 29), with one home run and six RBIs in the series. The A's beat the New York Mets, four games to three.
air reggie Home-run hitters tend to strike out a lot. Reggie certainly did. He is the all-time leader with 2,597 strikeouts in his career.

Reggie was Series MVP with the A's (top) and Yankees.

Great PLAYERS

Kirby Puckett

The Minnesota star led his team to Twin wins

Kirby Puckett was built more like a bowling ball than a big-league hitter. At 5' 8" and 220 pounds, Kirby was short and round. But when it came to delivering a big hit or making a key catch, the Minnesota Twins' outfielder was a giant.

Kirby helped the Twins win two World Series during his career. His biggest moments, though, came against the Atlanta Braves in 1991. Kirby became a real World Series hero that year.

The 1991 Series was one of the most exciting ever played. Five of the seven games were decided by one run. Three of the games, including the final two, went into extra innings.

The Twins won the first two games but lost the next three. Heading into Game 6, Kirby was angry at himself. Although he had hit a home run in Game 3, Kirby had batted just .167 over the first five games. Kirby knew he had to do better for Minnesota to win.

And Kirby did just that! In Game 6, he kept the Twins alive

Scouting REPORT

name Kirby Puckett
born March 14, 1961, Chicago, Illinois
career stats Hit .318 with 207 home runs and 1,085 RBIs over 12 seasons (1984–95) with Minnesota. Led the American League in hits four times. Led A.L. in RBIs in 1994, with 112. Won the league batting crown in 1989 with a .339 average.
world series stats Hit .308 with two homers and seven RBIs in two Series. Batted .357 with a team-high 10 hits in 1987.
neat feat In the sixth games of his two World Series, Kirby had seven hits in eight at-bats. That's an .875 average!

all by himself with one of the best performances in World Series history. That night, Kirby had three hits, three runs batted in, three runs scored, and a stolen base! He also sparkled in centerfield. In the third inning, he made a leaping catch against the outfield fence to rob Atlanta's Ron Gant of a home run.

But Kirby saved his best moment for the game's final pitch. It was the bottom of the 11th inning. The score was tied, 3–3. Kirby led off against Atlanta pitcher Charlie Liebrandt. He slammed Charlie's fourth pitch into the left-centerfield bleachers to win the game and tie the Series at three wins apiece. It was one of those magical home runs that change the tone of an entire Series.

Kirby trotted joyfully around the bases after he smashed his 1991 game-winner (far left).

The Twins beat the Braves, 1–0, in 10 innings the next evening to win the world championship.

You might say Kirby had a thing for sixth games of the World Series. In 1987, the Twins faced the St. Louis Cardinals in the Series. As in 1991, Minnesota fell behind, three games to two. As in 1991, Kirby kept his team alive almost by himself with a great performance. He had four hits in four turns at bat and scored four runs. The Twins won, 11–5, and won the championship the next day.

When it came to the World Series, Kirby was a giant, indeed.

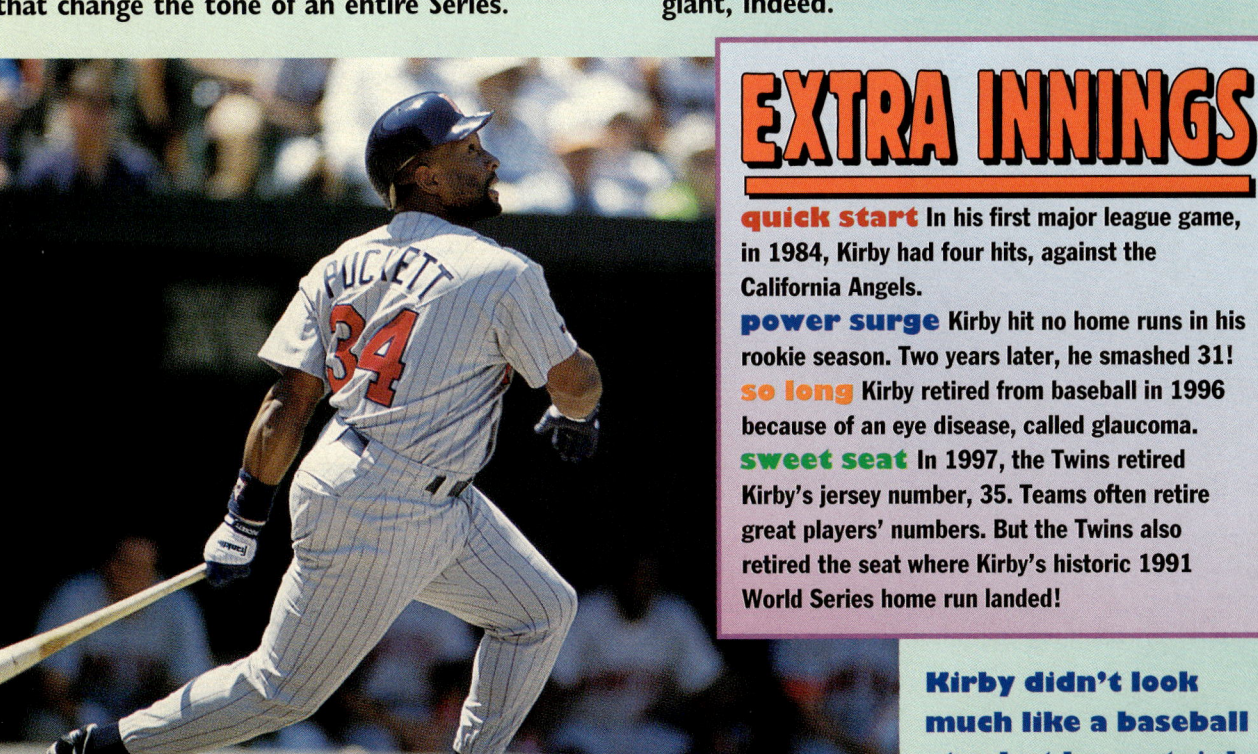

EXTRA INNINGS

quick start In his first major league game, in 1984, Kirby had four hits, against the California Angels.

power surge Kirby hit no home runs in his rookie season. Two years later, he smashed 31!

so long Kirby retired from baseball in 1996 because of an eye disease, called glaucoma.

sweet seat In 1997, the Twins retired Kirby's jersey number, 35. Teams often retire great players' numbers. But the Twins also retired the seat where Kirby's historic 1991 World Series home run landed!

Kirby didn't look much like a baseball star but he certainly played like one!

Joe Carter

His ninth-inning blast made baseball history

Millions of baseball players dream about doing it, but before Joe Carter, no one ever actually did it. On October 23, 1993, Joseph Chris Carter hit a come-from-behind home run in the bottom of the ninth inning to win the World Series. You can't be a bigger hero than that!

The Toronto Blue Jays led the Philadelphia Phillies, three games to two, in the 1993 World Series. But they trailed 6–5 going into the bottom of the ninth inning of Game 6, at the Toronto SkyDome. A win by the Phillies would force a seventh and deciding game. Two runs by the Jays, though, would make them the first team since the 1978 New York Yankees to repeat as World Series champions.

Relief pitcher Mitch Williams came in to protect the one-run lead for the Phillies. Mitch was nicknamed "The Wild Thing" because his pitching sometimes got very wild. Sure enough, Mitch walked Blue Jay outfielder Rickey Henderson on four pitches to lead off the ninth. Mitch retired the next Blue Jay batter, Devon White, on a fly to leftfield for the first out. But designated hitter Paul Molitor then slashed a single to centerfield. Now there were baserunners on first and second with one out.

Joe stepped into the batter's box. Joe was a power-hitting outfielder. He had hit 33 home

After his homer, Joe danced around the bases (left) and was raised on high.

Scouting REPORT

name Joseph Chris Carter
born March 7, 1960, Oklahoma City, Oklahoma
career stats (through 1996): Hit .261 with 357 home runs and 1,280 RBIs over 14 seasons (1983–1996) for the Chicago Cubs, Cleveland, San Diego, and Toronto. Five-time All-Star. Hit 30 homers six times.
world series stats (through 1996): Hit .271 with 4 home runs and 11 RBIs in two Series. Hit .280 with 2 homers and 8 RBIs in 1993 Series.
neat feat Joe has had 100 RBIs in one season nine times.

Great PLAYERS

Joe smacked Mitch's pitch into leftfield for a come-from-behind, Series-winning homer.

runs during the 1993 regular season. Joe was especially dangerous in pressure situations, and he was used to World Series pressure. In the 1992 Series, he had hit two home runs to help the Blue Jays beat the Atlanta Braves, four games to two.

But 89 World Series had been played before 1993. None of those Series had ever ended with a come-from-behind homer. Who expected that to happen now? Did anyone think that Joe would make history?

Joe worked the count to two balls and two strikes. Then, Mitch threw a fastball. Joe crushed it. The ball sailed over the leftfield fence for a home run. Joe had made history! He had hit a Series-winning, come-from-behind homer — the first ever.

The SkyDome crowd of 52,195 was treated to fireworks as Joe danced around the bases and crossed home plate. The Blue Jays were world champions again.

Joe Carter became a World Series hero forever.

EXTRA INNINGS

30-30 club Joe is one of only seven A.L. players to hit 30 or more home runs and steal 30 or more bases in the same season. He did it with the Cleveland Indians in 1987, when he had 32 homers and 31 stolen bases.

more valuable than that? Even with his famous home run, Joe wasn't named MVP of the 1993 World Series. That honor went to his Toronto teammate, Paul Molitor. Paul hit .500 (12 for 24), scored 10 runs, and finished with 24 total bases.

big hit Some 528 World Series games had been played before the sixth game of the 1993 World Series. Only one of those games had ended with a come-from-behind home run: Game 1 of the 1988 World Series. Kirk Gibson won that game for the Los Angeles Dodgers (see page 31). But Kirk didn't win the Series with his hit.

Tom Glavine

Tom's terrific pitching ended Atlanta's jinx

In the early 1990's, the Atlanta Braves seemed jinxed. Year after year, they had great teams. They won more games than any other team. They won three National League West championships. They played in two World Series.

But they never won the World Series. Until 1995. In 1995, pitcher Tom Glavine brought Atlanta its first world title by winning two games, including the decisive sixth game. Tom's one-hitter for eight innings in Game 6 was one of the best pitching performances in Series history.

The Braves faced the hard-hitting Cleveland Indians. The Indians had All-Stars Albert Belle, Kenny Lofton, and Carlos Baerga. Cleveland had led the American League with a hot .291 team batting average. In the A.L. championships, the Indians hit seven homers!

Scouting REPORT

name Thomas Michael Glavine

born March 25, 1966, Concord, Massachusetts

career stats (through 1996): Won 139 games, lost 92, with a 3.45 ERA over 10 seasons (1987–96) with Atlanta. Won Cy Young Award in 1991 with a 20–11 record and a 2.55 ERA.

world series stats (through 1996) 4–3 with 1.75 earned run average in four Series. Named MVP in 1995.

fun fact Tom was a terrific hockey player. The Los Angeles Kings chose him in the fourth round of the 1984 NHL draft.

No left-handed pitcher won more games than Tom from 1988–96.

Great PLAYERS

Tom won two games in the 1995 Series to give Atlanta the title.

But the Braves' pitchers stopped the Indians cold in the Series. Greg Maddux won the opener, 3–2. Tom allowed just two runs over six innings in Game 2, and the Braves won, 4–3.

Tom was even better in Game 6, with the Braves up three games to two. He used his great change-up pitch and pinpoint control to overpower Cleveland. No Indian batter got a hit in the first five innings!

In the top of the sixth inning, Cleveland's Tony Pena hit a bloop single. It was the only hit Tom gave up. In the bottom of the sixth, Brave slugger Dave Justice hit a solo home run. The Braves didn't need any more runs.

Tom struck out eight and walked three over eight innings. Relief pitcher Mark Wohlers pitched the ninth. He didn't give up a hit. The Braves were champions!

Tom was named MVP of the Series. In 14 innings, he had allowed only four hits and had a 1.29 ERA.

Even better, the Braves' Series jinx was finally over!

EXTRA INNINGS

leader of the pack Tom was baseball's winningest pitcher from 1991 through 1996, with 106 wins. He was the winningest *left-handed* pitcher from 1988 through 1996, with 137 wins.

the great glavine When he was in high school, Tom played hockey against future NHL stars Tom Barrasso and Kevin Stevens.

batman Tom has won three Silver Slugger Awards for batting. In 1996, he had a career-high 22 hits and a .289 (22 for 76) batting average. Tom has a .199 career batting average.

start me up In 1992, Tom became the first National League pitcher since Robin Roberts, in 1955, to start the All-Star Game two years in a row. Through 1996, Tom had been named to the N.L. All-Star team four times.

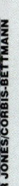

19

John Wetteland

The Yankee reliever saved game after game after . . .

The New York Yankees have had some of baseball's best relief pitchers over the years. Joe Page, Sparky Lyle, and many others played pivotal roles in helping the Yankees win world championships. But none of them did what John Wetteland did.

In the 1996 World Series, against the Atlanta Braves, John earned a World Series record four saves. And he did it in four games in a row! John's feat helped New York come back after losing the first two games of the Series to win the championship. It was the Yankees 23rd world title but only their first in 18 years.

John's most difficult save came in Game 5. New York was leading 1–0 in the ninth inning. Atlanta had a runner on third base with one out.

John came in from the bullpen to pitch to hard-hitting catcher Javier Lopez. He got Javier to ground out. Then he intentionally walked dangerous hitter Ryan Klesko. That was a risky move because it put the winning run on first base.

The Braves sent up Luis Polonia to pinch-hit. John threw his hardest and best stuff, but Luis fouled off six consecutive pitches. Finally, Luis hit a deep fly ball to right center. It looked as if

John shut down the Braves in Game 6 to clinch the Series.

Scouting REPORT

name John Karl Wetteland

born August 21, 1966, San Mateo, California

career stats (through 1996) Won 28 games, lost 33, with a 2.92 ERA and 180 saves over eight seasons (1989–96) with Los Angeles, Montreal, amd New York. Led A.L. in saves in 1996, with 43.

world series stats (through 1996) 0–0 with 2.08 ERA and four saves in one Series. Had six strikeouts and allowed one run and four hits in $4 \frac{1}{3}$ innings.

fun fact John plays the clarinet, guitar, and saxophone. His dad, Ed, is a professional piano player.

20

Great PLAYERS

John saved more games in one Series than any other pitcher in history.

it would fall in for a game-winning hit! But rightfielder Paul O'Neill raced over and caught the ball with a lunging grab. John had his third save and the Yankees had their third win.

In Game 6, John was called upon again by New York manager Joe Torre. This time he had a two-run lead to protect with three outs to go. If John could retire the Braves, the Yankees would win the Series.

John struck out Atlanta rookie Andruw Jones to start the inning. But then he gave up singles to Ryan Klesko and Terry Pendleton. Things were getting tense. Luis Polonia came in to pinch-hit again. John struck him out!

Now there were two outs and two men on base. Marquis Grissom slashed a run-scoring single to cut the Yankees, lead to 3–2.

EXTRA INNINGS

quick getaway Despite his Series heroics, John was not wearing a Yankee uniform when the 1997 season began. He signed as a free agent with the Texas Rangers in December 1996.

real relief John and Dave Righetti are the only Yankees to record 40 saves in a season.

super saver In 1996, John saved 24 games in 24 consecutive appearances. That broke the record of 19 straight, set by Lee Smith in 1993. John also struck out 69 batters in only 63 2/3 innings in 1996.

mvp John was only the second relief pitcher named MVP of the World Series. Rollie Fingers of the Oakland A's earned the honor in 1974. Rollie had a win and two saves against the Los Angeles Dodgers that year (see page 25).

John concentrated even harder. He got Mark Lemke to pop up in foul territory. Yankee third baseman Charlie Hayes charged over and caught the ball. The Yankees were champions!

John was named the Series MVP and earned a place in the record book as the greatest World Series closer in baseball history.

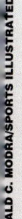

21

1950: Yogi tagged out Phillie Eddie Waitkus.

1996: Bernie blasted a big homer.

The Yankees

Winning the Series is a tradition

When Bernie Williams, John Wetteland, and company claimed the world championship for New York in October 1996, they were just carrying on a great Yankee tradition: winning the World Series. The Yankees have dominated the Series like nobody's business. They have played in 34 World Series and won 23 of them. No other team has won more than nine championships!

The Yankees have had many great teams over the years. But one dynasty stands out as the best of the best: the team that won every Series from 1949 to 1953. They won five straight! That's a record that may never be broken.

Five future Hall of Famers played during those years: outfielders Joe DiMaggio and Mickey Mantle, catcher Yogi Berra, pitcher Whitey Ford, and shortstop Phil Rizzuto. The manager was Casey Stengel, another Hall of Famer.

Billy Martin is famous for being a great Yankee manager. As a player, he was never great — except in the World Series.

Billy's career batting average over 11 big-league seasons was only .257. But in five World Series with the Yankees, he hit .333. In 1953, Billy tied a Series record with 12 hits. He also batted .500, with two homers and eight RBIs.

Billy helped save the 1952 Series with his fielding. Late in Game 7, he dashed in from second base to make a knee-high catch a few feet from home plate.

22

Great TEAMS

1951: Joe drove in five runs and hit a homer against the Giants in his last Series.

Casey told funny stories and was known as "The Old Professor." But he had a magic touch when it came to managing. He was good at platooning players. He would play mostly right-handed hitters against left-handed pitchers. He would load up on left-handed batters if a righty was pitching.

During the 1949–53 streak, the Yankees won an overwhelming 20 of 28 Series games. They beat the Brooklyn Dodgers three times and topped the Philadelphia Phillies and the New York Giants once each. The Cleveland Indians finally ended the streak by winning the American League pennant in 1954.

The Yankees have had great teams in nearly every decade. In the Series, they:

• won back-to-back titles in 1927 and 1928, when Babe Ruth and Lou Gehrig (see page 4) led the lineup known as "Murderers' Row";
• swept four straight Series from 1936–39, with Lou and Joe DiMaggio leading the way;.
• played in five Series in a row in the early 1960s, and won two of them (1961, 1962);
• beat the Los Angeles Dodgers in 1977 and 1978, behind sluggers Thurman Munson and Reggie Jackson (see page 12);
• and, finally, won their 23rd World Series in 1996!

Yogi Berra should be nicknamed Mr. World Series. The Yankee catcher played in more Series (14) than anyone else in history. He won more Series (10) than anyone. He is the all-time leader in games played and hits. He is second in runs and RBIs and third in home runs.

In the 1956 World Series, against the Brooklyn Dodgers, Yogi starred on both sides of the plate. He caught Don Larsen's perfect game in Game 5. As a batter, he smacked a grand slam in Game 2 and a pair of two-run homers in Game 7 to clinch the title. Yogi drove in 10 runs in the Series!

23

The Cardinals

St. Louis raced to three Series wins in the '40s

Stan won seven batting titles and played on three Series winners.

Zoom! There goes another base runner! The St. Louis Cardinals liked to put pressure on their opponents with speedy baserunning. In 1946, Enos Slaughter's gutsy baserunning helped them win a World Series!

But the Cards didn't win a world championship just because of Enos's mad dash from first base to home plate (see page 30). They were a great team. They had three future Hall of Famers: Enos, speedy second baseman Red Schoendienst, and oufielder Stan Musial, the best hitter in the National League. Infielders Whitey Kurowski and Marty Marion were among the best at their positions. The Cards had the best pitching staff in the National League, too. They won 509 games from 1942 through 1946. That's almost 102 victories per season!

The Cardinals also won three World Series in five years. In 1942, they handed the New York Yankees their first Series defeat since 1926. In 1944, they beat their crosstown rivals, the St. Louis Browns, in six games. Finally, they edged the Boston Red Sox in seven games in 1946. In that Series, pitcher Harry Brecheen won three games and had an 0.45 ERA, — and Enos ran all the way home.

In 1946, left-handed pitcher **Harry "The Cat" Brecheen** finished the regular season with a so-so record of 15 wins and 15 losses. But in the 1946 Series, Harry was anything but so-so.

Harry threw a four-hit shutout in Game 2, and a complete-game victory in Game 4. In the seventh game, he came in to pitch the final two innings and got his third win.

In three World Series, Harry had a 4–1 record with a 0.83 earned run average. His career ERA is the best in Series history.

Great TEAMS

Unexpected hero Gene slugged four homers in the 1972 Series.

The Athletics

Oakland's colorful crew cleaned up

The Oakland A's of the 1970s were as colorful as their green and gold uniforms. The team was full of strong personalities. Sometimes they battled one another almost as hard as they did their opponents.

On the field, though, the A's were as steady as a rock. They won three straight World Series titles, from 1972 to 1974. The New York Yankees are the only other team in history to win that many Series in a row.

The A's had an endless supply of stars. Sluggers Reggie Jackson, Sal Bando, and Joe Rudi led the offense. Pitchers Vida Blue, Jim "Catfish" Hunter, Ken Holtzman, and Rollie Fingers shut down opponents. Even the guys who weren't stars came through in the Series. In 1972, Gene Tenace (see box) led the A's over the Cincinnati Reds. In 1974, Bert Campaneris hit .353 against the Los Angeles Dodgers. (The A's beat the New York Mets in 1973.)

The A's streak ended in 1975. By then, they had made their mark as a truly great — and unforgettable — World Series team.

HERO

Slugger Reggie Jackson missed the 1972 Series with an injury. But the A's got all the power they needed to beat the Reds from an unexpected source: **Gene Tenace**. During the regular season, Gene was the back-up catcher. He hit only .225 with 5 home runs. In the Series, he smashed four homers, including two in his first two at-bats! For the Series, Gene batted .348 and was named MVP.

Gene never came close to those heroics again. He batted .147 in the three other World Series he played in. His career batting average was .241.

Great TEAMS

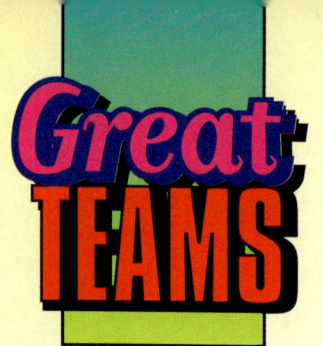

The Reds

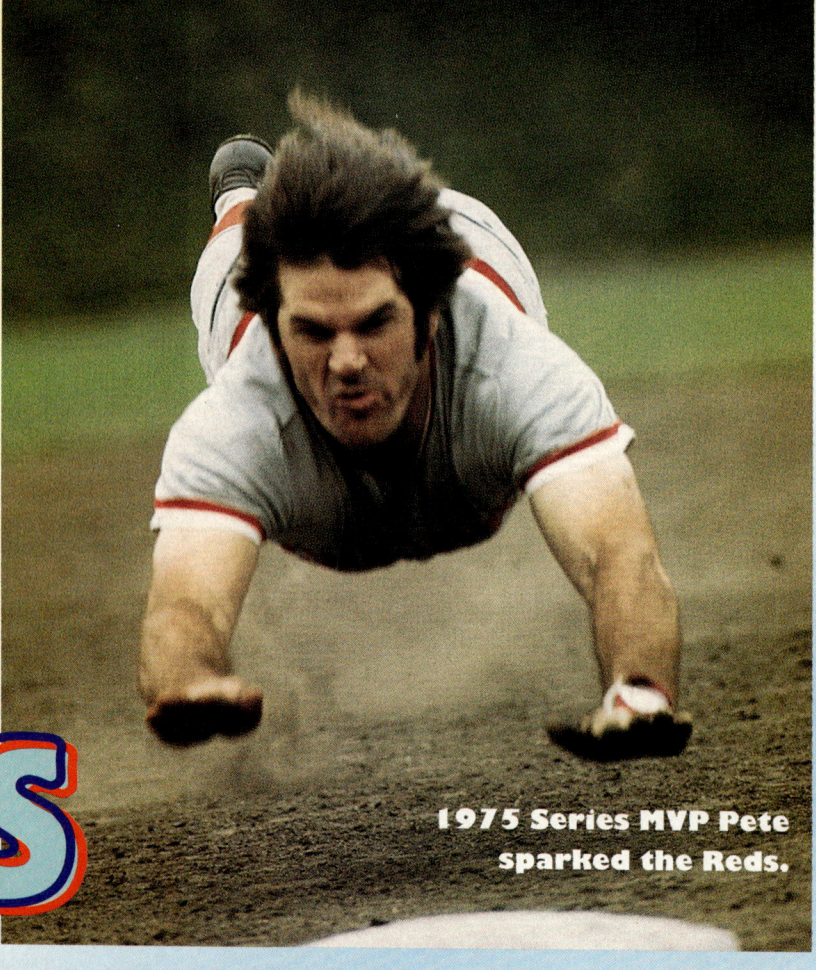

1975 Series MVP Pete sparked the Reds.

Cincinnati's Big Red Machine ruled

The Cincinnati Reds were known as the Big Red Machine because their powerful lineup seemed to mow down opponents. Pete Rose, Joe Morgan, and Ken Griffey, Senior, were terrific hitters who got on base a lot. Sluggers Johnny Bench, Tony Perez, and George Foster drove in tons of runs. Shortstop Dave Concepcion and centerfielder Cesar Geronimo were sensational fielders. Their wasn't a weak link in the lineup.

The Reds won back-to-back World Series. In 1975, they beat the Boston Red Sox in one of the finest Series ever played. Five of the games, including the famous sixth game (see page 27), were won by one run.

In 1976, the Reds swept the New York Yankees in four games, outscoring them 22–8. That win made them the first National League team to win consecutive World Series since the 1921–22 New York Giants. The Big Red Machine ruled!

HERO

Johnny Bench was a one-man gang in the 1976 World Series. He hit .533 with two home runs and six RBIs and was named Series MVP. He practically won Game 4 by himself. Johnny hit two home runs and drove in five of the Reds' seven runs that night! In the fourth inning, with the score tied, 1–1, he blasted a two-run homer to give the Reds the lead for good. His three-run homer in the top of the ninth inning put the finishing touches on a 7–2 victory.

HEINZ KLUETMEIER (TOP); DICK RAPHAEL/SPORTS ILLUSTRATED

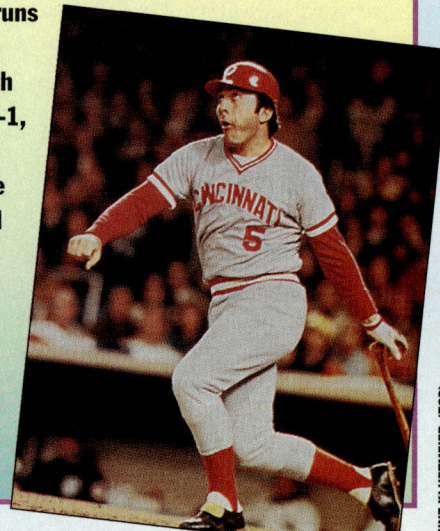

Great MOMENTS

Boston Classic

Scouting REPORT

name Carlton Ernest "Pudge" Fisk
born December 26, 1947, Bellows Falls, Vermont
career stats Hit .269 with 376 home runs and 1,330 RBIs over 24 seasons (1969–93) with Boston and the Chicago White Sox. Holds the major league record for home runs hit by a catcher, with 351.
world series stats Hit .240 (6 for 25) in 1975 Series. Led all players by drawing seven walks.
neat feat Carlton hit a major league record 72 home runs after he turned 40 years old. He retired at age 45.

It was well past midnight. Carlton Fisk, the Boston Red Sox star catcher, walked up to the plate. He was leading off the bottom of the 12th inning of Game 6 of the 1975 World Series.

The Red Sox and Cincinnati Reds were locked in one of the most exciting Series ever. The Reds had won three games. They needed just one more win. But Boston would not go quietly. The game was filled with awesome defensive plays and clutch hits. The Red Sox tied the score, 6–6, in the eighth.

Four innings later, Carlton was up, facing Reds reliever Pat Darcy. Carlton swung at the second pitch. He sent a high, arcing fly toward the left-field corner. It was hit far enough to be a home run. But would it stay fair or hook foul?

Carlton took two steps toward first and waved his hands as if he could direct the ball fair. The ball hit the foul pole for a home run, and an end to the four-hour battle.

Boston's 7-6 win tied the Series at three games apiece. The next night, the Reds took the Series, with a 4–3 win.

But Carlton's homer will forever be one of the great moments in World Series history.

1975 Carlton's 12th-inning smash put him into Boston's gallery of heroes.

Great MOMENTS

Perfect!

Umpire Babe Pinelli's hand shot into the air. Strike three! New York Yankee catcher Yogi Berra raced toward the mound. He hurled himself into pitcher Don Larsen's arms. The greatest pitching performance in World Series history was complete. It was perfect!

Don had been wild in Game 2 of the 1956 World Series. Yankee manager Casey Stengel started him in Game 5 anyway. Good move. On October 8, Don pitched the only perfect game in World Series history. Not one Dodger reached base.

Don had some close calls. In the second inning, Dodger star Jackie Robinson hit a hard grounder. The ball hit the third baseman's glove and bounced to shortstop Gil McDougald. Gil's throw to first base beat Jackie. In the fifth, centerfielder Mickey Mantle made a running one-handed catch of a deep fly ball.

By the ninth inning, the Yankees were winning 2–0. Don needed three more outs. He quickly retired Carl Furillo and Roy Campanella. Pinch-hitter Dale Mitchell was up. Don's first pitch was high. The next two were strikes. Then Dale fouled off a pitch. On the next pitch, Dale started to swing, then tried to stop. But umpire Babe Pinelli signaled strike three! Don had pitched his perfect game.

1956 Don (right) and Yogi hugged and jumped for joy after Don's perfect performance.

Scouting REPORT

name Don James Larsen
born August 7, 1929, Michigan City, Indiana
career stats Won 81 games, lost 91, with a 3.78 earned run average over 14 seasons (1953–67) with 8 teams. 11–5 with a 3.26 ERA in 1956.
world series stats 4–2 with a 2.75 ERA in five Series. His perfect game was the first one since 1922, when Charlie Robertson of the White Sox beat the Tigers, 2–0.
fun fact Don was nicknamed "Gooneybird" because he didn't take many things seriously.

Home Run Hero

1960 Bill ran into a crowd of excited teammates and fans after his game-winning hit.

It may be the most famous home run in World Series history. And it was hit by a man who was known for his fielding, not his bat.

Bill Mazeroski was one of the best second basemen ever to play baseball. In 1960, his great fielding helped the Pittsburgh Pirates get to the World Series. There, they faced the powerful New York Yankees.

It was a tight Series. Each team won three games to force a seventh-game showdown, in Pittsburgh. Game 7 was wild. The lead went back and forth between the teams. After 8 ½ innings, the score was tied, 9–9.

Bill led off for the Pirates in the bottom of the ninth. The Yankee pitcher was Ralph Terry. Ralph led the Yankees in strikeouts that season. Ralph's first pitch to Bill was a ball. The next pitch was a high fastball. Bill swung. The ball went soaring over the ivy-covered wall in leftfield! Home run! The Pirates won the game, 10–9, and the Series. It was their first world championship in 35 years.

As Bill skipped around the bases, he was surrounded by a mob of happy Pirate fans who had run onto the field. He had to make his way through the fans just to touch home plate. When he did, Bill became the first man ever to win a World Series by hitting a home run in the bottom of the ninth inning.

He became a true World Series hero.

Scouting REPORT

name William Stanley "Maz" Mazeroski

born September 5, 1936, Wheeling, West Virginia

career stats Hit .260 with 138 home runs and 853 RBIs over 17 seasons (1956–72). Won 8 Gold Gloves.

world series stats Hit .308 (8 for 26) in two Series. Hit .320 in the 1960 Series.

fast fact In 1966, Bill set the major league record for double plays by a second baseman in one season. He turned 161.

Great MOMENTS

1946 Safe! Enos slid across home plate while Boston catcher Al Partee fielded the throw. Cardinal star Marty Marion watched.

Scouting REPORT

name Enos Bradsher "Country" Slaughter
born April 27, 1916, Roxboro, North Carolina
career stats Hit .300 over 19 seasons (1938–59) with four teams. Led the National League in batting (1942), in RBIs (1946) and in triples, twice.
world series stats Hit .291 (23 for 79) in five Series. Played on four championship teams: the Cards in 1942 and 1946 and the Yankees in 1956 and 1958.

Mad Dash

Enos Slaughter was not known for being a fast runner. He had only 71 stolen bases during his 19-season major league career. But in 1946, the St. Louis Cardinal rightfielder won the World Series with his legs.

The Cardinals and the Boston Red Sox each won three games. After 7½ innings of Game 7, the score was 3-3. Enos led off the bottom of the eighth with a single. Two outs later, Enos was still on first. Harry Walker was up. The Cardinals took a risk. They put on a hit-and-run play. That meant Enos would start running as soon as the pitcher threw the ball.

Harry hit a line drive into left-centerfield. Enos was already past second base when centerfielder Leon Culberson got to the ball. Leon threw to shortstop Johnny Pesky. Johnny hesitated. Then he saw Enos racing toward home plate. He couldn't believe that Enos was trying to score on the play!

Johnny threw the ball home. Too late. Enos scored. With his mad dash, Enos won the game and the Series for the Cardinals!

Dodger Drama

The Los Angeles Dodgers had a problem. It was Game 1 of the 1988 World Series and their most valuable player, outfielder Kirk Gibson, was hurt. Kirk had injured one leg and re-injured the other during the National League Championship Series. When he woke up before the first World Series game, he had trouble swinging a bat. How could he play?

Without Kirk, the Dodgers seemed to have little chance against the Oakland A's. The A's had sluggers Jose Canseco and Mark McGwire. They had star pitchers Dave Stewart and Dennis Eckersley. Even with Kirk, they would be tough to beat!

After 8½ innings of Game 1, the Dodgers trailed 4–3. In the ninth inning, Dennis, the A's relief ace, retired the first two batters easily. Then he walked Mike Davis. The Dodger pitcher was due to hit next. L.A. manager Tommy Lasorda needed a pinch-hitter. He chose Kirk.

Kirk limped slowly to the plate. Dennis got two strikes. The next three pitches were balls. Then Dennis threw a slider. Kirk swung . . .

crack!

The ball flew into the rightfield bleachers for a two-run homer. Dodgers win, 5–4! Kirk hobbled around the bases, punching his fist into the air.

That was Kirk's only appearance in the Series, but it inspired the Dodgers. They won the Series in five games.

1988 Crack! Despite his aching body, Kirk clobbered the ball in Game 1.

Scouting REPORT

name Kirk Harold Gibson
born May 28, 1957, Pontiac, Michigan
career stats Hit .268 with over 17 seasons (1979–95) with four teams. Named N.L. MVP in 1988 when he batted .290 with 25 homers and 76 RBIs.
world series stats Hit .368 (7 for 19) in two Series. Helped Detroit win the 1984 world championship by hitting .333 with two home runs and seven RBIs.
cool fact: Kirk was a college football star at Michigan State University.

The Catch

Great MOMENTS

Cleveland Indian slugger Vic Wertz had been killing the New York Giants all day. Now it was the eighth inning of Game 1 of the 1954 World Series. The score was Cleveland 2, New York 2, with two men on base.

Vic was up. He had already had three hits in the game. Giant manager Leo Durocher brought in lefty reliever Don Liddle to face Vic, a lefty. But on Don's first pitch, Vic hit a soaring line drive to the deepest part of centerfield at New York's Polo Grounds. It looked like an extra base hit.

Willie Mays, the Giants' star centerfielder, turned and raced furiously into deep centerfield. He ran with his back to home plate. He ran and ran. Then, some 450 feet away from home plate, he stuck out his glove and caught the ball over his shoulder, like a football pass.

Willie whirled around. He launched a bullet throw back to the infield to keep the runners from advancing. Willie's great play kept Cleveland from scoring.

In the 10th, Giant Dusty Rhodes hit a three-run homer to win the game. New York swept Cleveland in four games.

Scouting REPORT

name Willie Howard Mays
born May 6, 1931, Westfield, Alabama
career stats Hit .302 with 660 home runs and 1,903 RBIs over 22 seasons (1951 to 1973) with the Giants and New York Mets. Hit 40 or more homers six times. Named N.L. MVP in 1954 and 1965.
world series stats Hit .239 (17 for 71) with six RBIs in four World Series (1951, 1954, 1962 and 1973). His catch is considered the greatest fielding play in World Series history.
cool fact Willie is the godfather of San Francisco Giants star Barry Bonds.

1954

Willie's catch looked almost impossible. But he felt it was no big deal. "I had it all the way," said Willie.